Gay People of Color: Facing Prejudices, Forging Identities

by Jaime A. Seba

Mason Crest Publishers

MASON CREST PUBLISHERS INC.
370 Reed Road
Broomall, Pennsylvania 19008
(866)MCP-BOOK (toll free)
www.masoncrest.com

First Printing
9 8 7 6 5 4 3 2 1

Library of Congress Cataloging-in-Publication Data
Seba, Jaime.
  Gay people of color : facing prejudices, forging identities / by Jaime Seba.
      p. cm.
  Includes bibliographical references and index.
    ISBN 978-1-4222-1748-1 (hbk.)   ISBN 978-1-4222-1758-0 (series)
    ISBN 978-1-4222-1877-8 (pbk.)   ISBN 978-1-4222-1863-1 (pbk. series)
  1. Minority gays—Juvenile literature. I. Title.
  HQ76.26.S433 2011
  306.76'608900973—dc22
                        2010019189

Produced by Harding House Publishing Service, Inc.
www.hardinghousepages.com
Interior design by MK Bassett-Harvey.
Cover design by Torque Advertising + Design.
Printed in the USA by Bang Printing.

PICTURE CREDITS

Creative Commons: pp. 31, 38
Darnell, Ervan; Creative Commons: p. 55
Georgia House of Representatives: p. 34
Haynes, Charles; Creative Commons: p. 56
Hinkel, Keith; Creative Commons: p. 16
Hood, Adrian; Creative Commons: p. 29
Krauss, Diane; Creative Commons: p. 19
Logo Films: p. 49
PR Photos: p. 10
Sikander, Seher; Creative Commons: p. 42
Stitt, Jason; Fotolia: p. 45
Sykes, Bev; Creative Commons: p. 24
Terwilliger, Jessie; Creative Commons: p. 23
Thompson, Christy; Fotolia: p. 13
U.S. National Archives: p. 27
Winder, Mark; Fotolia: p. 46
Zesmeralda; Creative Commons: p. 58

Contents

Introduction

We are both individuals and community members. Our differences define individuality; our commonalities create a community. Some differences, like the ability to run swiftly or to speak confidently, can make an individual stand out in a way that is viewed as beneficial by a community, while the group may frown upon others. Some of those differences may be difficult to hide (like skin color or physical disability), while others can be hidden (like religious views or sexual orientation). Moreover, what some communities or cultures deem as desirable differences, like thinness, is a negative quality in other contemporary communities. This is certainly the case with sexual orientation and gender identity, as explained in *Homosexuality Around the World*, one of the volumes in this book series.

Often, there is a tension between the individual (individual rights) and the community (common good). This is easily visible in everyday matters like the right to own land versus the common good of building roads. These cases sometimes result in community controversy and often are adjudicated by the courts.

An even more basic right than property ownership, however, is one's gender and sexuality. Does the right of gender expression trump the concerns and fears of a community or a family or a school? *Feeling Wrong in Your Own Body*, as the author of that volume suggests, means confronting, in the most personal way, the tension between individuality and community. And, while a community, family, and school have the right (and obligation) to protect its children, does the notion of property rights extend to controlling young adults' choice as to how they express themselves in terms of gender or sexuality?

Changes in how a community (or a majority of the community) thinks about an individual right or responsibility often precedes changes in the law enacted by legislatures or decided by courts. And for these changes to occur, individuals (sometimes working in small groups) often defied popular opinion, political pressure, or religious beliefs. Some of these trends are discussed in *A New Generation of Homosexuality*. Every generation (including yours!) stands on the accomplishments of our ancestors and in *Gay and Lesbian Role Models* you'll be reading about some of them.

One of the most pernicious aspects of discrimination on the basis of sexual orientation is that "homosexuality" is a stigma that can be hidden (see the volume about *Homophobia*). While some of my generation (I was your age in the early 1960s) think that life is so much easier being "queer" in the age of the Internet, Gay-Straight Alliances, and Ellen, in reality, being different in areas where difference matters is *always* difficult. Coming Out, as described in the volume of the same title, is always challenging—for both those who choose to come out and for the friends and family they trust with what was once a hidden truth. Being healthy means being honest—at least to yourself. Having supportive friends and family is most important, as explained in *Being Gay, Staying Healthy*.

Sometimes we create our own "families"—persons bound together by love and identity but not by name or bloodline. This is quite common in gay communities today as it was several generations ago. Forming families or small communities based on rejection by the larger community can also be a double-edged sword. While these can be positive, they may also turn into prisons of conformity. Does being lesbian, for example, mean everyone has short hair, hates men, and drives (or rides on) a motorcycle? *What Does It Mean to Be Gay, Lesbian, Bisexual, or Transgender?* "smashes" these and other stereotypes.

Another common misconception is that "all gay people are alike"—a classic example of a stereotypical statement. We may be drawn together because of a common prejudice or oppression, but we should not forfeit our individuality for the sake of the safety of a common identity, which is one of the challenges shown in *Gay People of Color: Facing Prejudices, Forging Identities.*

Coming out to who *you* are is just as important as having a group or "family" within which to safely come out. Becoming knowledgeable about these issues (through the books in this series and the other resources to which they will lead), feeling good about yourself, behaving safely, actively listening to others *and* to your inner spirit—all this will allow you to fulfill your promise and potential.

James T. Sears, PhD
Consultant

chapter 1

Who Are Gay People of Color?

A t the annual San Francisco Pride Festival, thousands of people gather to celebrate the lesbian, gay, bisexual, and transgender (LGBT) communities.

The parade features hundreds of organizations, including some often-overlooked members of the LGBT rainbow: the NAACP, Asian & Pacific Islander Wellness Center, South Bay Queer and Asian, Gay Vietnamese Alliance, Queer Latina/o Arts Collective, and Bay Area American Indian Two-Spirits.

The organizations provide support for "people of color," a term that has come to refer to individuals who are not Caucasian or white. In the LGBT community, these are the individuals who are often represented the least in media and entertainment. They are the minority within the minority.

According to a study by the Gay and Lesbian Alliance Against Defamation, only sixteen of six hundred television series' regular characters (3 percent) on the major networks in the 2009–2010 television season are lesbian, gay, or bisexual.

Of those, only four are people of color.

So if you don't know any gay people, and you don't see any gay people on television who look like you, how can you relate to them?

Openly gay comedian Wanda Sykes is one of the few black public figures who are willing to speak openly about being gay or lesbian. She recognizes that a lack of understanding of LGBT issues among African Americans leads to more destruction and hurts the overall black community.

"If you live in your little community and you don't know gay people and you don't know that we're lov-

Wanda Sykes is one of the few publically gay people who is also a person of color.

ing people and we all want the same things, then you won't be able to identify with them or care about that other group," said Sykes. "Speaking from the people I know, it's tougher for a black person to come out (than a white person). Then again, I'm sure there's some white people from the **Bible Belt** who have been disowned from their families and have had a hard time. There's such a **stigma** about being gay (in the black community) that a lot of the men don't want to be labeled as gay, so they live straight lives, and then, behind closed doors, they're fooling around with men, bringing HIV home to their wives. We're literally killing ourselves over this fear of homosexuality."

Sykes, who married her partner in 2008 and came out publicly later that year, was referring to being on

What's That Mean?

The *Bible Belt* refers to the American South, an area where conservative Christians make up a large part of the population.

Stigma is a mark of shame.

EXTRA INFO

The Gay and Lesbian Alliance Against Defamation (GLAAD) is an organization that works to stop the spread of negative, usually false, information that could harm members of the LGBT community.

the "down low," a term used to describe black men who have physical relationships with other men while still maintaining they are straight and involved with women.

"Sadly, intolerance of gays in the black community is everywhere, but the place where I have witnessed it the most has been within the churches," said Sameerah Blue, who works to support her friends in Hollywood's gay community. "A lot of the churches in the black community preach from a very **conservative** place. . . . It's not uncommon to hear sermons declaring homosexuality an **abomination** and sickness in the eyes of God. These types of sermons don't just begin and end with the Christian churches of the black community, they can be found in the **spectrum** of faiths that the black community is involved in, from Christian, to Jehovah's Wittiness' and the Nation of Islam. Black churches all over the country are teaching their flock intolerance of the gay community within the black community."

For a culture that has traditionally relied so heavily on religion for personal guidance, she says the

What's That Mean?

Someone or something that is *conservative* likes things to stay the way they've always been.

An *abomination* is something that causes extreme disgust and hatred.

A *spectrum* is a wide variety.

People of color who are people of faith—and also members of the LGBT community—often struggle to reconcile their various identities.

attitude of churches can make it even more difficult for gay people to accept themselves.

"One of the things that I find most disturbing about the church fostering this kind of intolerance is

that there are a lot of people within the black gay community that would love nothing more than to be able to lean on the people in their churches when they are subjected to the hate and intolerance that they run across in the rest of their world," she said. "The churches' views take a place that should be nurturing and supportive and turn it into just another closed door."

Likewise, many gay black men and women fear how their families will respond, and ultimately don't want to risk the effect that coming out could have.

"The reason that so many young black men aren't so *cavalier* about announcing their sexual orientation is because we need our families," said Glenn Ligon, an openly gay black artist. "We need our families because of economic reasons, because of racism, because of a million reasons. It's the idea that black people have to stick together, and if there's the slightest possibility that coming out could disrupt that, guys won't do it."

EXTRA INFO

Keith Boykin, an African-American journalist, describes "the black church" as the most homophobic institution in the black community. But also the most "homo-tolerant." This is a major contradiction in the life of black church congregations. People may nod and say "Amen" in agreement with the pastor's "hell and damnation" approach to homosexuality, but in reality, Boykin says, gays and lesbians are everywhere in the church. "Many of our black churches would stop running if the gay, lesbian and bisexual members dropped out. That's why nobody ever asks them to leave. Instead they beat them down in the hopes that the gay members will not become strong enough to challenge their own oppression. The black church has a 'don't ask, don't tell' policy about homosexuality. And quite frankly, the religious bigotry in the black church is killing us as a people. It is killing the people who are dying of AIDS because the church won't talk to them candidly about sexuality. And it is killing the people who are dying in the streets because they feel morally authorized to regulate public expressions of homosexuality."

These concerns about disrupting the family are also what can keep many Latino people from coming out, according to Lourdes Torres, president of Amigas Latinas, a lesbian and bisexual support group. "The family is the unit that provides the support and the one place that people can feel free and protected,"

Perez Hilton is a well-known gay Cuban-American, famous for his celebrity gossip website.

said Torres. "It becomes doubly difficult for people to come out."

Of the more than 43 million people of Latin-American heritage in the United States, about four million are gay. One of the most well known openly gay Latinos in American popular culture is Perez Hilton, a Cuban-American who runs his own celebrity gossip website. He understands the struggle Latino families go through with gay and lesbian loved ones, because he went through it with his own family. "At the beginning, when I came out to my mom, she reacted with a sigh and said, 'You're my son and I have to love you,'" Hilton said. "But now she says, 'You're the best son in the world, and we need to find you a man.'"

Hilton's experience reflects a shift in the Latino community's attitudes toward greater acceptance of homosexuality. *El Diario La Prensa*, one of the oldest and largest Spanish-language newspapers in America, recently endorsed the rights of same-sex couples to marry.

"A lot of walls are starting to crumble," said Charlie Vazquez, a New York-based author whose fiction has appeared in books such as *Best Gay Love Stories: NYC*. "We're at a crossroads," he says. "A new generation of better-educated Latinos is coming of age." This has helped gay and lesbian Latino youth to be more accepting of themselves. According to a 2007 survey by the Gay, Lesbian and Straight Education

Network (GLSEN), more than half of gay Latino students participate in Gay-Straight Student Alliances in schools that have these organizations. "While harassment in schools for Latino gay students remained high, we also know that these students have more support than in past generations," said Elizabeth Diaz, a senior researcher for GLSEN.

According to a report by the Association of Gay and Lesbian Psychiatrists (AGLP), for LGBT people in communities of color, issues of accepting sexual orientation can often conflict with their racial or ethnic identity. If your culture doesn't acknowledge that homosexuality exists, then how can you be both gay and a member of the cultural community? ("There are no gays in our community, therefore you are not Black, Asian, Arab, etc."). In a similar way, the LGBT community may focus significantly more on sexual identity and disregard cultural identity. If you are both gay and a person of color, how do you pull together these two vital pieces of your identity?

Hyeouk Chris Hahm, Assistant Professor at the Boston University School of Social Work, has studied ethnic and sexual identities among Asian Pacific Islander (API) teens. "In the Western gay and lesbian community, 'coming out,' is a final revelation that you are homosexual, while for API in America of Korean descent, there is 'coming home,' where you want to integrate culturally and be both an American and Korean," said Professor Hahm. This can be

Actor George Takei, from the cast of the original Star Trek *and an openly gay Asian American, has done his part for both the Asian American and LGBT communities.*

incredibly complicated for API teens, who are then faced not only with the threat of being rejected by their friends, families, and community, but also of losing their ethnic identity. They are forced to choose one identity over the other.

Considering the complex issues facing people of color in the gay community, it becomes even more important to have role models who are not just gay, but who are able to also embrace and claim their ethnic identity. Unfortunately, examples of such role models are not easy to find. But they are out there.

Poet and scholar Paula Gunn Allen wrote about lesbian and gay history in Native American culture. Indian-born LGBT rights *activist* Urvashi Vaid was named one of *Out* magazine's fifty most powerful gay and lesbian people in America. And while few in number, LGBT people of color appear on some of television's most popular shows, including Callie Torres on *Grey's Anatomy*, Angel Garcia on *Mercy*, Oscar Martinez on *The Office,* and Angela Montenegro on *Bones.* Such representatives—even the fictional ones—are necessary to offer hope for young people of color who are faced with **homophobia** in their communities on a daily basis.

Hilton is optimistic that the time for hate and intolerance is coming to an end. "It's tough—I'm not saying it's not there," he said. "But as time goes on, it will change."

FIND OUT MORE ON THE INTERNET

Asian/Pacific Gays and Friends
apgf.org/

Black LGBT People, Invisible No Longer
www.lgbtpov.com/2010/02/the-black-lgbt-manifesto-invisible-no-more/

Latino/Latina Gay Civil Rights
www.unitycoalition.org/

READ MORE ABOUT IT

Asencio, Marysol. *Latino/a Sexualities: Probing Powers, Passions, Practices, and Policies*. Piscataway, N.J.: Rutgers University Press, 2010.

Johnson, E. Patrick. *Sweet Tea: Black Gay Men of the South, An Oral History*. Chapel Hill, N.C.: University of North Carolina Press, 2008.

chapter 2

The Politics of Being a Minority in the Minority

I n the days before the 2008 election, voters received telephone calls that featured the voice of then-Presidential candidate Barack Obama.

"I believe marriage is a union between a man and a woman," Obama's recorded voice said. "Now, for me as a Christian, it is also a sacred union. God is in the mix."

Then a narrator told them to vote in favor of California's Proposition 8, also known as the Marriage Protection Act, which would change the state's constitution to define marriage as being between a man and a woman. The measure would *negate* a state Supreme Court ruling earlier in the year that legalized same-sex marriage.

What's That Mean?

To *negate* is to reverse and invalidate a decision.

Something that is *unprecedented* is different from anything that has happened before.

On Election Day, an ***unprecedented*** number of black voters turned out to overwhelmingly support Obama in his successful bid to become the nation's first African American president. And initial exit polls showed that 70 percent of black voters in California had also voted in for Proposition 8—despite the fact that Obama had actually publicly stated his opposition to the same-sex marriage ban.

"One cannot underestimate the effect that . . . the robo-calls had where people heard Barack Obama's voice and then they were told to vote yes on 8," said

Voting Yes on Proposition 8 meant that "only marriage between a man and a woman is valid or recognized in California."

This Californian couple had been waiting thirty-one years for the right to marry.

Kate Kendell, Executive Director of the National Center for Lesbian Rights.

Later analysis of voting data revealed that the percentage of black voters supporting Proposition 8 was closer to 60 percent, which was still significant for a measure that passed with only 52 percent of the vote.

"We took a huge leap forward and then got dragged twelve feet back," said black lesbian comedian Wanda Sykes, who married her partner just days before Proposition 8 passed. "I felt like I was being attacked, personally attacked. Our community was attacked. . . . Like, hey I'm sitting here living my life and suddenly the government—the people, really—walked in the door to our living room and said, 'No, you're not allowed to do this.' And that's frightening."

The passing of Proposition 8 was a blow to gay rights in California, which had recognized the marriage of 18,000 same-sex couples in the six months before the measure was passed. In that same year, similar measures banning gay marriage also passed in Florida and Arizona.

"I know that's the reason so many black people voted, because they wanted to see a black person in office," said Brian Jones, an openly gay black man who lives in Los Angeles. "I think most black people are saying, 'Why do gay people want to get married?'

but it's the same thing [as the civil rights struggle]. Anybody who wants to get married should be able to get married. It's funny how many black people have forgotten about how oppressed we were at one point."

While only 42 percent of all Californians attend church regularly, one study shows that 57 percent of black voters in California attend church at least once a week. And 70 percent of those weekly churchgoers supported Proposition 8.

EXTRA INFO

The Three-Fifths Compromise was an agreement between Southern and Northern states reached during the Constitutional Convention in Philadelphia in 1787 in which three-fifths of the population of black slaves would be counted in the U.S, Census for purposes of distributing taxes and determining the number of members of Congress a state would qualify for (since representation in Congress is based on a state's population). It increased the power of Southern slave states by allowing them to count slaves, who could neither vote nor paid taxes, as a part of their population. In a sense, it defined the value of black people as being three-fifths the value of white people. After the Civil War (1861–1865), black people were counted "in full" in census reports.

Many people see gay rights as an extension of the civil rights movement begun by Martin Luther King Jr.

"I think it's mainly because of the way we were brought up in the church; we don't agree with it," black voter Jasmine Jones told the *Washington Post* after the election. "I'm not really the type that I wanted to stop people's rights. But I still have my beliefs, and if I can vote my beliefs that's what I'm going to do. God doesn't approve it, so I don't approve it. And I approve of him."

The bottom line for many black voters was that they did not see a connection between the modern-day struggle for gay rights and the push for black civil rights in the latter half of the twentieth century.

"What the church does is give that perspective that this is a sacred issue as well as a social issue," said Derek McCoy, African American outreach director for the Protect Marriage Campaign. "The reason I feel they came out so strong on the issue is one, for them, it's not a civil rights issue. It's a marriage issue. It's about marriage being between a man and a woman and it doesn't cut into the civil rights issue, about equality. The gay community was never considered a third of a person."

But not all black leaders agree that gay rights are separate from civil rights. Many have considered the battle for gay equality to be an extension of the black civil rights

What's That Mean?

An *icon* is a person who is highly respected as the best representative of something positive.

movement, including Coretta Scott King, wife of civil rights *icon* Reverend Dr. Martin Luther King, and Dorothy Height, the activist who died in April of 2010 at the age of ninety-eight.

"Civil rights are civil rights," said Height when she was honored in 1997 at the Human Rights Campaign National Dinner. "There are no persons who are not entitled to their civil rights. . . . We have to recognize that we have a long way to go, but we have to go that way together."

In April of 1993, LGBT activist Urvashi Vaid addressed a massive crowd at the March on Washington and recognized the place of the gay rights movement in America's history.

Activist Dorothy Height expressed her belief that gay equality is a part of the entire civil rights movement.

"We, you and I, each of us, we are the descendants of a proud tradition of people asserting our dignity," said Vaid. "It is fitting that the Holocaust Museum was dedicated the same weekend as this March, for not only were gay people persecuted by the Nazi state, but gay people are indebted to the struggle of the Jewish people against bigotry and intolerance. It is fitting that the NAACP marches with us, that feminist leaders march with us, because we are indebted to those movements."

Ron Buckmire, head of the Barbara Jordan/Bayard Rustin Coalition for black gay rights, feels this message was lost in the campaign leading up to the 2008 election. And he took the Proposition 8 results to be a sign that increased work must be done to bring awareness to the black community.

"The civil rights of people should not be put to a vote," he said. "Period. I would have thought that that message would have gotten through."

For some, a different message got through. *YO! Youth Outlook*, an award-winning literary journal of youth life that covers everything from substance abuse to racial issues and popular culture, reported that the passing of Proposition 8 served as a wakeup call for young people in the gay community who felt that the black community was being unfairly **stigmatized** as anti-gay.

"As one of many black people who opposed Prop 8, it's kinda scary that there's this group of people who were so willing to turn against black people," said twenty-year-old Terry Taplin, an African American poet nationally recognized for his advocacy of LGBT causes. "At the same time, there are a lot of homophobic sentiments in the black community that now are hard to deny."

But those sentiments aren't limited to the black community. In California, 53 percent of the Latino vote—the same percentage as white voters—and 49 percent of Asians also came out in favor of Proposition 8.

What's That Mean?

If something is *stigmatized* it is thought of in a very negative way and avoided.

LGBT activist Urvashi Vaid.

EXTRA INFO

Hate crimes are illegal acts, often violent, in which the victim is selected because of his or her race, religion, or sexual orientation. According to FBI statistics, there were well over 1,000 such crimes against LGBT people reported in 2009—but estimates for the actual number of violent crimes against people identified as gay are much higher since many states do not legally recognize "gay hate crimes" as a separate category and many gay people are, for many reasons, afraid to report them. The Matthew Shepard Hate Crimes Prevention Act is an act of the United States Congress that was passed on October 22, 2009 and signed into law by President Barack Obama on October 28, 2009. Named in honor of a young man brutally murdered in a hate crime in Wyoming in 1998, the act expands the 1969 United States federal hate-crime law (which protected victims of hate crimes based on race or religion) to include crimes motivated by a victim's actual or perceived gender, sexual orientation, gender identity, or disability. The act gives federal authorities, like the FBI, greater authority to investigate hate crimes motivated by homophobia and provides funding for state and local law enforcement to pursue and prosecute those who commit these crimes. The act is the first federal law to extend legal protections to LGBT victims of hate crimes

"I wasn't surprised by the Latinos," said Steve Smith, senior consultant for "No on 8." "Basically, Latinos and the Anglo population were fairly close. The **outlier** of the proposition was African Americans. Many are churchgoing; many had ministers tell them to vote."

The response from the Latino community matched the trends that had been occurring in Latin America in the years leading up to the election. Andres Duque, a founder of the Latino gay rights **coalition** Mano a Mano, feels that Latinos are often depicted as being homophobic. But in reality, much progress has been made. Same-sex civil unions are legal in Uruguay, Buenos Aires, and Mexico City, and in 2007, Colombia approved a bill to grant gay couples the same rights to social security benefits as straight couples.

"We have actively campaigned to get the media in the United States to move on from the stereotypes of Latin America being too **machismo**, homophobic,

What's That Mean?

An **outlier** is a portion of the results of a vote that is farthest from the average.

A **coalition** is an organization that is made up of other organizations, all united in the same cause.

Machisimo refers to the very tough and masculine behavior that is traditionally highly valued in the Latino community.

and Catholic to ever approve gay rights measures," said Duque, who is Columbian.

Other trends indicate that minority groups in the gay community are being recognized and accepted. Despite the apparently backward steps among black voters in California in 2008, the following year Simone Bell became the first openly lesbian African American state legislator in U.S. history when she was elected to the Georgia State House of Represen-

Simone Bell was the first openly lesbian African American to be elected as a state legislator.

tatives in 2009; Georgia voters also sent Alex Wan to the Atlanta City Council, the first openly gay man and the first Asian-American to fill a seat in that body.

And despite the rocky beginning, President Obama also demonstrated his commitment to supporting gay rights in his first eighteen months in office. He supported the passage of hate crime legislation, he encouraged the repeal of

the "Don't Ask, Don't Tell" policy that prohibits gay people from serving openly in the military, and the White House even hosted the first Gay Pride Day celebration. And in 2010, he mandated that hospitals extend visitation rights to the partners of gay men and women, a huge step in expanding the rights of gay Americans.

"The election of Mr. Obama brings hope to so many people in so many ways . . . but I think for the gay community of color it means an extension of the civil rights that our parents and grandparents fought for in the '60s," said Sameerah Blue, an LGBT rights advocate and supporter of Obama's campaign. "Back then it was the right to vote and ***desegregation*** of the country as a whole. Now it's the fight to make sure that everyone has access to all civil rights across the board regardless of race or orientation. If President Obama can push forward the repeal of 'Don't Ask Don't Tell' and finally legalize gay marriage throughout the country, the work to put him into office will have been worth it."

FIND OUT MORE ON THE INTERNET

Icons of the civil rights movement now speak out for same-gender marriage equality
www.soulforce.org/article/766

Black voters and Proposition 8
themoderatevoice.com/24204/stop-scapegoating-black-people-for-proposition-8/

The growing movement for gay rights in Latin America
www.foreignpolicy.com/articles/2009/02/17/gays_in_latin_america_is_the_closet_half_empty

READ MORE ABOUT IT

Rimmerman, Craig. *The Politics of Gay Rights.* Chicago, Ill.: University of Chicago Press, 2000.

Williams, Juan. *My Soul Looks Back in Wonder: Voices of the Civil Rights Experience.* New York: Sterling Publishing, 2004.

chapter 3

Health Issues

E. Lynn Harris self-published his book *Invisible Life* in 1992. The novel told the story of a masculine young black man who was devoted to his girlfriend, but was also strongly attracted to other men. He faced the difficult issues of being black and gay, which seemed impossible to navigate.

Though fictional, the story struck a chord with readers. After the book was picked up by a publisher, it went on to sell nearly a half million copies.

"I was surprised by the reaction to my book," Harris said. "People were in such denial that black men could be doing this. Well, they were doing it then, and they're doing it now."

The behavior his book described is something that has come to be known as being on the "down low" ("DL"). Black men would have romantic relationships with women, but also engage in sexual activity with men. This meant leading a double life and creating the image of being straight.

"Any time you foster a **subculture** that encourages people to lead a double life, you can't count on them to use common sense and protect themselves," said Sameerah Blue, who has known people who engage in this behavior. "Because the small piece of latex that can save their lives is also what could give them away."

She alludes to the idea that many men in this lifestyle believe that something as simple as using a condom means acknowledging that they are gay. And that's something they can't handle and avoid at all costs.

What's That Mean?

A *subculture* is a group of people who share a lifestyle that is different and separate from the larger majority.

When data began showing that more and more black women who weren't IV drug users were becoming infected with HIV, people began to take a closer look at why that was happening. Though some women may have been infected by male drug users, experts recognized that men engaging in unprotected sex with other men could then be infecting their female partners.

"To me, it's a dangerous cop-out," said Emil Wilbekin, the black and openly gay editor in chief of *Vibe* magazine. "I think you have to love who you are, you have to have respect for yourself and others, and to me most men on the DL have none of those

Emil Wilbekin, an openly gay black man, was the editor in chief of Vibe *magazine from 1999 to 2004, and went on from there to become the editor of* Giant *magazine and then* Essence.

qualities. There's nothing sexy about getting HIV, or giving it to your male and female lovers. That's not what being a real black man is about.''

To Chris Bell, an HIV-positive black man from Chicago who often speaks at colleges about sexuality and AIDS, this is an unfair **generalization**. He feels that relating HIV to being on the down low made closeted gay black men the "modern version of the highly sexually dangerous, irresponsible black man who doesn't care about anyone."

The term, which became popular in the 1990s by singers such as R. Kelly and TLC, is about secrecy. And that need to keep silent about being gay is what really put black men at risk. As Bell pointed out, black men had been infected with HIV long before it started to impact straight black women. But that was rarely acknowledged.

"There was a real sense in black communities that you had to put your best face forward in order to prove that you deserve equal rights and equal status, and that face didn't include gays and IV drug users with AIDS," said Cathy Cohen, author of *The Boundaries of Blackness: AIDS and the Breakdown of Black Politics*. "It's been a very slow process for the black leadership in Amer-

What's That Mean?

A *generalization* is an opinion on a larger issue formed by just a few examples.

EXTRA INFO

In August 2005, three weeks before his nationally televised declaration that "George Bush doesn't care about black people," Kanye West made a statement he'd later describe as braver and more difficult than his attack on the White House. Hip-hop, he told MTV, was supposed to be about "speaking your mind and about breaking down barriers, but everyone in hip-hop discriminates against gay people. ... I wanna just come on TV and just tell my rappers, tell my friends, 'Yo, stop it.'" West spoke again on the subject in a November 2005 interview, discussing his love for his openly gay cousin, not to mention his conflicted but changing attitude toward his interior decorator. West's call for tolerance remains one of the highest-profile criticisms of gay bashing and homophobia that hip-hop has seen. Homophobic lyrics and attitudes remain a disturbing theme in hip-hop and rap music, despite growing criticism and the rising careers of a small number of openly gay rappers.

ica to own up to this disease. Not acknowledge it in passing, but own it."

According to John Peterson, a professor of psychology at Georgia State University who specializes in AIDS research among black men, gay people in the black community have difficult choices when it comes to living their lives openly.

"**Mainstream** gay culture has created an alternative to mainstream culture," he said. "Many whites take advantage of that. They say, 'I will leave Podunk and I will go to the gay barrios of San Francisco and other cities, and I will go live there, be who I really am, and be part of the mainstream.' Many African-Americans say, 'I can't go and face the racism I will see there, and I can't create a functioning alternative society because I don't have the resources.' They're stuck."

Hip-hop superstar Kanye West has spoken out against his genre's gay bashing.

Many decide not to risk being ***ostracized*** from their families and communities, and instead remain hidden in the closet. And even for the individuals who don't engage in dangerous sexual behavior, there are still other health issues. Some turn to alcohol or drugs as a way to cope with their internal conflicts.

"The choice becomes, do I want to be discriminated against at home for my sexuality, or do I want to move away and be discriminated against for my skin color?" he said.

Substance abuse issues aren't limited to the black gay community. Studies have found that Asian Pacific Islander men and women who are gay face pressure from a culture that focuses on traditional family values. Not adhering to these standards can bring shame on the family and community. These factors led to gay men and women in the API community having a higher prevalence of tobacco use, binge drinking, marijuana use, and other drug use.

In a similar way in the Latino community, fears of homophobia and not being accepted have kept many gay men from seeking necessary medical treatment, including HIV testing. In 2007, Latinos in New York State represented 16 percent of the population, but accounted for 30 percent of people living with HIV/AIDS. And many tested late in their infection, meaning they missed out on critical treatment, according to a report by the Latino Commission on AIDS that was released in 2010.

"This report calls attention to the stigma associated with HIV/AIDS and the need to combat the homophobia and **transphobia** that discourage Latinos and many others from talking openly about and getting tested for HIV," said New York City Council Speaker Christine C. Quinn.

Being afraid and staying hidden in the closet can be damaging in many other ways. Emanuel Xavier, a gay poet and spoken-word artist, saw how people in the Latino community reacted to gay people. He even witnessed other kids throwing stones at a gay Latino hairdresser. And the Roman Catholic priests who were held in the highest esteem regularly condemned homosexuality.

What's That Mean?

Transphobia is the fear of and prejudice against members of the transgender community, people who identify with and often behave as the gender other than the one they were born.

Even after he realized his sexual orientation, he knew his friends and neighbors would never accept him for who he was. When she learned he was gay, his own mother called him names. He couldn't handle it.

The result was not a surprise, nor was it at all uncommon. He began using and selling drugs, and he engaged in dangerous sexual behavior, just like many other young people he knew.

Cultures that value "machismo" and "tough" forms of masculinity are sometimes uncomfortable with homosexuality. Gay people who belong to these cultures often find it hard to be open about their identities.

"I became all those things society expected me to become," Xavier said. "I thought that was the only thing I could be."

Eventually he realized he was risking his life. He got clean, and refocused his life and energy on his art and advocating for the rights of LGBT Latinos.

"Fortunately, I walked away unscathed," he said. "I thought that God had given me a second chance, and I felt like I had to do something with that."

Many gays who are people of faith find comfort and strength in the belief that God accepts them as they are, even if the church does not.

FIND OUT MORE ON THE INTERNET

The "down low" and HIV/AIDS
www.cdc.gov/hiv/topics/aa/resources/qa/downlow.htm

Gay Asian and Pacific Islanders
www.gapa.org/

Latina Lesbians
www.amigaslatinas.org/

READ MORE ABOUT IT

Costa, Maria Dolores. *Latina Lesbian Writers and Artists.* New York: Routledge, 2003.

King, J.C., Karen Hunter. *Beyond the Down Low: Sex, Lies, and Denial in Black America.* New York: Random House, 2004.

chapter 4

Forging Ahead

Four friends explore life and love in the big city. They support each other in tragedies and share the tales of their romantic misadventures.

It sounds like the plot of the popular series *Sex and the City*. But this time, there's a twist.

The four friends are black gay men. And the drama of their lives included homophobia, HIV, gay bashing, and same-sex marriage.

For two seasons, viewers of *Noah's Arc* followed the highs and lows of Noah, Alex, Ricky, and Chance in the dramatic comedy on Logo, a gay cable television network.

"It's a good way for some minority kids to see that black people can integrate into society very easily without anything happening," said Brian Jones, an openly gay man living in Los Angeles, where the show is also set. "It's a way to show gay people of color that it's okay to be gay. It's about love and relationships. It's a good way to put it out there."

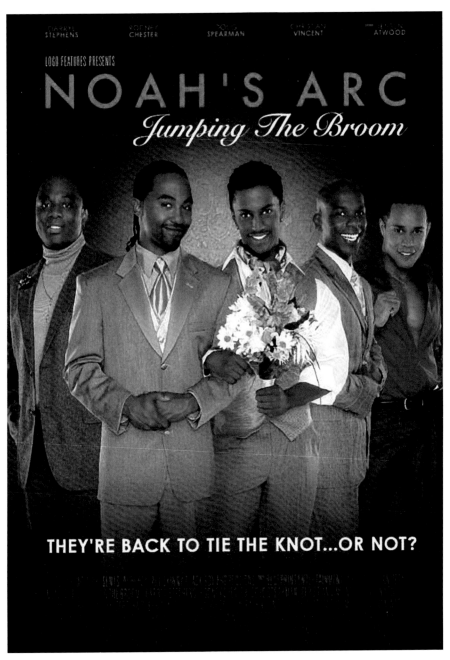

In 2008, Jumping the Broom, *a movie based on the television show* Noah's Arc, *was released. It won the GLAAD (Gay & Lesbian Alliance Against Defamation) award for best feature film.*

Noah's Arc is part of a trend of more ***inclusive*** images in the gay community. Logo features a lineup of gay-themed shows, many of which include people of color. *RuPaul's Drag Race*, a reality competition for drag queens, largely features black, Asian, and Latino contestants. And it's hosted by famed drag queen RuPaul, also known as openly gay black actor RuPaul Andre Charles.

While RuPaul's ***flamboyant*** television personality isn't representative of most gay people in communities of color, having high-profile role models on television helps establish the gay community as being more than just white.

What's That Mean?

Something that's *inclusive* brings together people of all kinds.

Flamboyant refers to something or someone that's colorful and attention-getting.

"There are probably like two more (gay black role models) than there ever were before," Jones joked. "But even if it's straight women who are gearing their music toward gay kids, like Lady Gaga and Madonna, that helps."

Of the few black celebrities who are public about their homosexuality, some of the most notable have come out after living typical "straight" lifestyles.

Olympic gold medalist Sheryl Swoopes was the star of the WNBA women's professional basketball league. She led her team to four league champion-ships and earned three regular-season MVP awards. She was also the first female athlete to have a shoe named after her, when Nike released the Air Swoopes. When Swoopes was pregnant, the WNBA splashed her image on promotional posters and marketing campaigns designed to depict the league and its players as straight, to counteract rumors that the league was largely gay.

"The talk about the WNBA being full of lesbians is not true," Swoopes said. "There are as many straight women in the league as there are gay. What really irritates me is when people talk about football, baseball, and the NBA, you don't hear all of this talk about the gay guys playing. But when you talk about the WNBA, then it becomes an issue. Sexuality and gender don't change anyone's performance on the court."

But in 2005, several years after her divorce, Swoopes publicly came out.

"My reason for coming out isn't to be some sort of hero," said Swoopes. "I'm just at a point in my life where I'm tired of having to pretend to be somebody I'm not. I'm tired of having to hide my feelings about the person I care about. About the person I love."

Swoopes revealed that she was in a relationship with former Old Dominion basketball coach Alisa Scott.

"Some people might say my coming out after just winning the MVP award is heroic, and I understand that," she said. "And I know there are going to be some negative things said, too. But it doesn't change who I am. I can't help who I fall in love with. No one can.

Still, giving young people the opportunity to see that a sports icon—a woman who had been called the "female Michael Jordan"—as a successful, proud gay woman helps counteract a sea of intolerant messages.

Former NBA star Tim Hardaway's made headlines with a hate-laced public *diatribe* after his fellow pro basketball player John Amaechi came out in 2007.

EXTRA INFO

In 1993 Sheryl Swoopes, playing for Texas Tech University, scored a record 47 points in a national championship game. After college, Swoopes competed internationally, and in 1996 she won an Olympic gold medal as part of the U.S. team (she also won gold medals in 2000 and 2004). She was among the first women drafted in 1997 to play professional basketball for the WNBA, signing with the Houston Comets. She helped lead the Comets to a "fourpeat" of consecutive championships in 1997, 1998, 1999, and 2000, and she has consistently been one of their best players. Swoopes was also voted the league's Most Valuable Player in 2000, 2002, and 2005.

Homophobic themes are also common in hip-hop and rap music.

Homophobic themes are common in hip-hop and rap music. "You can often hear it in the lyrics of mainstream rap artists," said Sameerah Blue. "Whenever there is a beef or something negative needs to be said about another rapper, they start in calling one another 'fags.' While most of this may be **hyperbolic**, there are a lot of kids that can't distinguish an entertainer's real views, for the characters that they play to sell albums."

On the opposite end of the spectrum, Mexican pop singer Christian Chavez, lead singer of the band RBD, publicly came out in 2007.

"He wasn't rejected by any of his band mates or fans," openly gay gossip columnist Perez Hilton said. "That's a huge step for gay visibility in the Latino media world."

At the time when Chavez came out, Puerto Rican singer Ricky Martin publicly supported him. In 2010, Martin also acknowledged that he is gay.

"At the end of the day you're dealing with a very personal and private issue," Rob Halford, openly gay singer for heavy-metal act Judas Priest, said of

What's That Mean?

A *diatribe* is angry or abusive speech or writing.

Hyperbolic refers to language that is highly exaggerated and extreme.

Martin's coming out. "What he did was incredibly important for himself and the Latino community."

Though it had been rumored in the entertainment industry for years, it took time for Martin to speak about it in public. But in the end, he saw it was about being true to himself, just as Swoopes had.

"Discovering I'm gay just sort of happened much later in life," Swoopes said. "I'm a firm believer that when you fall in love with somebody, you can't control that."

Comedian Wanda Sykes had a similar experience. Although she knew she was gay, she also knew she wouldn't be accepted. So she married record producer David Hall.

"I actually made the choice to be straight as a kid," she said. "Early on I knew (being gay) wasn't gonna fly. No way. And from the teachers and church and all it was, 'This is wrong! What's wrong with me?' And you pray and ask God to take it away, and you bury it and bury it, and you shut that part of yourself off. Then you try to live the life that you're supposed to live."

Even after she came out to herself and the people in her life, she still kept her personal life private, including her marriage to her partner, Alexandra. But when she looked around at the many other black men and women struggling with living their lives openly, she began to wonder if she had more of a responsibility.

"I wrote the checks and signed the petitions and did all that, but could I have done more?" she asked herself.

So she contacted an acquaintance, out gay black actor Doug Spearman, one of the stars of *Noah's Arc*. She remembered that he served on the Board of Directors for Equality California, a gay rights advocacy group.

"I had no idea Wanda was gay," Spearman said. "But she is a huge hero of mine—as an actress, as a comedian, and as a working black person."

Spearman helped Sykes to consider the benefits and pitfalls of being an out actor. A few days later,

Doug Spearman at the 2007 San Francisco Gay Pride Parade.

Margaret Cho is known for her stand-up routines where she critiques social and political problems, especially those pertaining to race, sexuality, and sex. She has won awards for her humanitarian efforts on behalf of women, transvestites, Asians, and the LGBT community.

she announced her marriage at a rally in Las Vegas. She later saw it in a news report on CNN and recognized how far-reaching the impact of her announcement could be. So she joined the board of Equality California.

"The role models in the gay community of color aren't going to be found on TV. They are found in the community leaders that run Bienestar and other outreach centers," said Blue, referring to the agency that provides AIDS/HIV and drug and alcohol prevention services to the Latino community. "The people that run these organizations help provide the people in the gay community of color a place to go for help and the support that they may not get from the community. Sadly, there are not enough of these outreach centers in the black community."

The most influential cultural icons are the ones who use their high profiles to draw attention to community causes. Comedian Margaret Cho has been recognized by the Gay and Lesbian Alliance Against Defamation, the Asian American Legal Defense and Education Fund, and the Lambda Liberty Aware for her extensive work in support of women, Asians, and the LGBT community. She also used her influence in a series of commercials urging people to vote against California's Proposition 8, which banned same-sex marriage in the state.

Tony Award-winning openly gay actor B.D. Wong has chaired AIDS Walk events and has been a supporter of the Family Equality Council. And George Takei, the former *Star Trek* star who married his long-time partner in 2008, has been recognized for his work in human rights and has been actively involved with the Japanese-American National Museum.

Many gay celebrities feel the responsibility to give back to their communities because they know what other people of color go through when they face the realities of being out.

"In the black American community, homophobia is rampant," said Director Lee Daniels. "I think it is

George Takei in the 2006 Chicago Gay and Lesbian Pride Parade.

very difficult to be out, gay, and black. I feel very much alone, especially amongst my people. It's a very lonely place."

Daniels, who is openly gay, became the first African American Director to be nominated for an Academy Award in 2010 for his film *Precious: Based on the Novel Push by Sapphire*. The heart-wrenching story of an abused young black girl included a minor storyline in which she found support and safety in her lesbian teacher's welcoming home. Though the gay plot was a very minor part of the story, it highlighted that the compassion and kindness shown by the individuals was far more important than their sexual orientation.

"Slowly but surely I have noticed more tolerance of gays within the community," said Blue. "Most of these changes seem to have occurred because the young people in the gay community of color have begun to work on changing the stereotypes that most people have of gay people, proving that they are loving, caring productive members of the community."

FIND OUT MORE ON THE INTERNET

Bienestar
www.bienestar.org

George Takei
www.georgetakei.com

Living Out Loud with Darian
loldarian.blogspot.com/2008/08/young-black-gay-in-america.html

Margaret Cho
www.margaretcho.com

READ MORE ABOUT IT

Endean, Steve. *Bringing Lesbian and Gay Rights into the Mainstream.* New York: Routledge, 2006.

Halpin, Mikki. *It's Your World—If You Don't Like It, Change It: Activism for Teenagers.* New York: Simon Pulse, 2004.

Huegel, Kelly. *GLBTQ: The Survival Guide for Queer and Questioning Teens.* Minneapolis, Minn.: Free Spirit Publishing, 2003.

Wright, Kai. *Drifting Toward Love: Black, Brown, Gay, and Coming of Age on the Streets of New York.* Boston, Mass.: Beacon Press Books, 2008.

BIBLIOGRAPHY

"The 4th Annual Power 50." *Out*, April 14, 2010.

Blake, John. "Gay Latino Americans Are 'Coming of Age.'" CNN, September 23, 2009.

Bolcer, Julie. "Video Salute to Women in LGBT Politics." *The Advocate*, April 1, 2010.

Boston University Medical Center. "Understanding The Process Of Homosexual Identity Formation Among Asian And Pacific Islander Youth." *Science Daily,* July 14, 2009.

Cane, Clay. "Precious Things: Lee Daniels and Gabourey Sidibe." *BET*, November 6, 2009.

Denizet-Lewis, Benoit. "Double Lives On The Down Low." *The New York Times*, August 3, 2003.

DiMassa, Cara Mia and Jessica Garrison. "Why Gays, Blacks Are Divided on Prop. 8." *Los Angeles Times,* November 8, 2008.

Granderson, LZ. "Three-Time MVP 'Tired of Having to Hide My Feelings.'" *ESPN: The Magazine,* October 27, 2005.

Johnson, Jason B. "Secret Gay Encounters of Black Men Could Be Raising Women's Infection Rate." *The San Francisco Chronicle*, May 1, 2005.

Jojola, Lloyd. "Indian Writer Led Groundbreaking Work in Native Literature." *Albuquerque Journal,* June 10, 2008.

Karpel, Ari. "Black and Gay Like Me." *The Advocate*, March 2009.

ABOUT THE AUTHOR AND THE CONSULTANT

Jaime A. Seba's involvement in LGBT issues began in 2004, when she helped open the doors of the Pride Center of Western New York, which served a community of more than 100,000 people. As head of public education and outreach, she spearheaded one of the East Coast's first crystal methamphetamine awareness and harm reduction campaigns. She also wrote and developed successful grant programs through the Susan G. Komen Breast Cancer Foundation, securing funding for the region's first breast cancer prevention program designed specifically for gay, bisexual, and transgender women. Jaime studied political science at Syracuse University before switching her focus to communications with a journalism internship at the Press & Sun-Bulletin in Binghamton, New York, in 1999. She is currently a freelance writer based in Seattle.

James T. Sears specializes in research in lesbian, gay, bisexual, and transgender issues in education, curriculum studies, and queer history. His scholarship has appeared in a variety of peer-reviewed journals and he is the author or editor of twenty books and is the Editor of the *Journal of LGBT Youth*. Dr. Sears has taught curriculum, research, and LGBT-themed courses in the departments of education, sociology, women's studies, and the honors college at several universities, including: Trinity University, Indiana University, Harvard University, Penn State University, the College of Charleston, and the University of South Carolina. He has also been a Research Fellow at Center for Feminist Studies at the University of Southern California, a Fulbright Senior Research Southeast Asia Scholar on sexuality and culture, a Research Fellow at the University of Queensland, a consultant for the J. Paul Getty Center for Education and the Arts, and a Visiting Research Lecturer in Brazil. He lectures throughout the world.